The Tanzanian Pressure Cooker

The life of a modern disciple, a missionary in Tanzania; his witness expressed in a tradition of friendship through letters

M. V. Southworth

For my sweet sister Mary LaPointe Engin, we had a blast when Mark visited.

"Greater love has no one than this, that one lay down his life for his friends."

John 15:13

Table of Contents:

Mark Day

Part I

Mark Day

Many moons ago, I was in a musical group that toured in the Eastern United States as well as abroad in Spain. The group was "Up With People". It was a year of song, dance and travel staying with over 88 families in the course of a year. Moreover, in the cast of just over 100 participants from all over the world, deep and everlasting friendships were forged. This is the story of one of those friendships.

Mark Day was from Monroe, Connecticut. Mark loved cows. He was a dairy specialist having graduated from the University of Connecticut. Mark took a year out of college to travel to tour with 'Up With People'. That is where I met

Mark. It was January of 1979 that we began our year first training at North Florida State College in Madison, Florida.

We learned the songs, the dances and steps that led to a dynamite two-hour show. Music is the universal language meant to bridge gaps and draw people from all walks of life together. The audience would participate and leave with a feeling of great satisfaction and an added incentive to go out and do good.

There are all sorts of personalities in such a group. I found myself gravitating towards a few. While I liked everyone, there were some with whom I was more comfortable.

The very first person who I met happened to be on the same airplane that I was on from New York to Tallahassee. That was Patricia Murphy. She had flown to New York from Belfast, Northern Ireland. She still recalls me asking the flight attendant, "Is there a bathroom on the airplane?"

I think Patricia thought I was a boisterous American as I ended up having to stay in the Days Inn motel alone upon arrival. Patricia roomed with Laura Howard, a gal from Tennessee.

However, it was Patricia with whom I grew closest. There was also a very sweet gal from Texas. Her name is Christy Wade. She was adorable and I liked her instantly. Add to the mix, Mark Day. Mark was a likeable, down-to-earth and unassuming fellow. He had a great sense of humor. Well, we all did. It was rather necessary for this year of intense travel and being away from home in the tender years of one's late teens.

Mark had the same color of eyes like my mother – between brown and green. I guess you call it hazel-colored eyes. His manner was gentle. He was not particularly tall, and he was of a slight to medium build. Mark had brown hair and a nice smile with good teeth.

Mark attended the United Church of Christ. He corresponded regularly with his pastor.

Mark was very frugal. He would write letters on scraps of paper napkins or wrappers.

I remember attending the Boston Pops with Mark as we were given tickets when we were in Beantown. We both pretended to "put on the dog". We talked with English accents. Mark went out of his way to get me a tin of pastilles during the intermission. I still have that tin that once held citrus flavored pastilles.

Mark was fun and easy to be around. He was rather like a brother to me. I think he was smitten with a redhead from Canada anyway in our group.

I remember our last show that we did in the Canary Islands. Mark let me take his place in the dance number. I was never out front though one of the staff said that I was good about filling in the blank spots on stage. Mark showed me the steps and I had my three minutes of fame. Even though it was the last show, the dance instructor was not amused. This was after all, a surprise stunt. Mark was humble. He did not care about being out in front.

The year ended in December of 1979. It was bittersweet. However, true friendships remained.

Mark returned to college after our tour ended. He lived in his car, a small Pinto, the following Summer. He was working in Old Sturbridge Village in Massachusetts. Mark was always conserving, and this was one of the ways to do that. He folded the back seat down and with the front seat pushed up against the steering wheel, he slept in a vertical position. He wrote in a letter to our mutual friend Christy Wade Lamb,

"I learned how blessed we really are and how much we really don't need in our lives. I also learned how it must be like to be a vagrant. There are a lot of them around. It has made me more sensitive to those that don't have a home or a secure place to go to. I think of the Cambodians and the boat people especially. But there are a lot of Americans as well. I am lucky, because for me it was a game. I could have at any time stopped playing it and found an apartment or gone home to my parents. Also, I was living in a car. Most people don't have that. So, it was a blast. But it was hard, too. I learned a lot."

29 January 1980 A.D.

Dear Mark,

Hi! I was so pleased with your letter and your thoughtfulness to remember me and send me the picture – not one, but two. They are just fine. Thank you, Mark.

My box still has not arrived from Spain. So, I have not got my film developed yet. But when I do, I will see if I can find some pictures of interest for you. I will never forget how you helped me out with lending me film or finances.

Have you got Dianne's autograph, woops, I mean address!? I would love to write to her.

I am writing with an old-fashioned desk pen. For example, you will note the ink blotch here – just like John-boy on the Walton's. You know how I want to be an authoress. Guess what Mark – I got a new electric typewriter for Christmas! I am so excited about it.

Grampa say hi and he was glad to hear you ask for him.

I just have to chuckle and with a tear when I think of you Mark. Remember the Pops concert in Boston, and our surprise 'I Got Rhythm' dance number. I will always think of you when I see a COW! Your sense of humor is unmatched! Our innocence, cough, cough! I just miss you and I think the world of you Mark. I admire your Faith.

I am currently taking winterim courses: Consumerism, Theatre – I got the lead in two one-act plays in my town. I will resume classes at North Country Community College Spring semester. I will be taking: Art Appreciation, Newswriting, Anthropology, Speech-Communications, Sociology, and slimnastics. I babysit in the interim, write on my new typewriter, work on my independent project (slide presentation, scrapbooks, journal, etc.).

Christmas was beautiful for me Mark and I am glad it was for you too Mark – especially with your family.

I will have to see that Muppet movie. I did see 'In Search of Historic Jesus' which I liked very much.

Congratulations with your job. Why that is quite an honor! Oh yes, I hope to work part-time in a department store come March.

Here is my cast evaluation Mark.

May God Bless you even more.

My love,

Virginia

FREE SAMPLE
sunrise®
instant SURPRISE
Nestlé
sunrise®
instant
mellowed with LOVE

Here is one of the first letters that I received from Mark after our tour. It was a makeshift card, and he had a pull tab to pull out the letter that was enfolded. He had recycled this cardboard packet that a free sample of Sunrise coffee had come in. He substituted the word "Surprise" for "Coffee", and he added the word "Love" after "Mellowed with".

Dear Virginia,

I got your beautiful card the other day, and boy, did you cheer me up! It sure has been a long time, eh, Virginia? But it was like yesterday that we were together in UWP.

You sound very busy and very happy. I'm really glad for you! Whenever I think of you Virginia, I can't help but smile. You are such a super person - a sincere one at that!

I have been busy finishing up school. You are now reading a letter from a college graduate! I bet you could tell by the great writing ability – so much different than my past letters! I am

glad it's over, but boy, now I have to think about reality, and no way am I ready for that! Augh!

School has kept me pretty busy. I was living with an elderly couple. I worked for my room and board, so it was pretty cost efficient. That's a college graduate word for "cheap". I'm still the same cheap old self!

They were a neat couple. The doctor, an MD, was 80 and had been practicing in town for 50 years! Can you imagine! I can't even imagine being 50 years old! But I tell you, they had more on the ball than I do. They were so active going here and there. Mrs. Gilman was funny because she was the real "mom" type. She would tell me what was good for me and be real charitable with her advice. Boy, she acted about 30 or something! But they are a laugh. I really enjoyed working for them. It took me a while to get used to them though. I missed farm work and milking the cows a lot. The

Gilman's had me rake leaves, vacuum, and stuff that was pretty much menial labor. It bored me, but I got used to it. I have my whole life to milk cows.

I have been kind of active in the Peace Movement. I don't like the idea of being blown out of the world. I guess not too many people do. I went to a March in Washington to protest the involvement in El Salvador. It was an experience, that is for sure. For one thing, everyone there was real negative about everything. Down with this, Down with that. They practically wanted to tear down society and start over. They saw little hope. I think "Hope" is a big word that we need to keep in our minds and in our hearts. So, with everyone yelling and being real childish, a friend and I decided to go sightseeing. We are not the dedicated types I guess. But it was a real blast. I think there are more constructive ways to promote peace.

I have not heard from too many folks in the cast. I wrote to Pat Murphy, but I have not heard back yet. I assume that she is doing well. I pray for her in such times of unrest.

I heard from Christy Wade. She is doing good – she is a fellow "aggie" – studying soil and plant science.

I think Dianne is working for a Dairy company as a secretary.

Matt has been doing some acting. I think he even won an award! It is amazing where time has gone.

I am gonna have to go now Virginia. Please send me your German address! I will be in Germany myself! I will be in Bavaria working on a farm this Summer. Boy, if we could get together! I will enclose my address, okay? Please, Please, write and tell me! Maybe I can teach you to milk one of those “brown eyed beauties”!!

Virginia, thank you so much for your super note. You really are special. I hope to hear from you.

Love, always

Mark

July 4th, 1981

Independence Day

(especially for Ticonderoga!)

Dear Virginia!

Hi! How are you? I do hope you got my letter before you left back to Germany. I was talking to Christy Wade and she sent me your address. I too, am in Germany! I am working on a dairy farm, of course, and loving it immensely.

My family here are super. They are so open, friendly and generous. They like to laugh a lot. I do too, so we get a long great. I work about 60 hours a week which leaves little time to do much else.

I am about 50 km west of Munich and 90 km from the Alps. It is really beautiful here. Actually, it reminds me much of Wisconsin. Had I known that I could have gone to the big Dairy Land in the states and saved a lot of money. Then, I would have missed out on all this culture – like Corn Flakes for breakfast and McDonald's in Munich. I guess it is hard to get away from good ole' Americana. But then, I'm really not trying to.

I am only here until September 3rd on a "Traineeship". That's a clever way of getting people to work on farms without having to pay too much money. I am making 500 DM, plus room and board for the whole summer. It is okay, because I really do love it here.

So, how about you?! Where are you? I am hoping we can get together before I go back. Do you realize it has been 1 and a half years since the "Good ole UWP days"? We two innocent- face types should try and get together. How is your job here? How long were you in Ticonderoga for? I hope that your grandfather is doing well. How long are you planning on staying in Germany? What are your future plans?

Virginia, I really enjoyed the letter you sent me from your home in Ticonderoga. Since we are so close here in Germany, we should see each other!

Well, I hope to hear from you. I hope you are doing well.

God Bless You,

Love,

Mark

P.S. – The post card is a picture of our house here in Grafrath! (O.K., O.K., so it is not exactly true!)

The post card was of a beautiful government building with pillars and a statue out front.

Mark's host family's home – not really!

A Tradition of Friendship

Mark and I corresponded regularly. I visited Patricia in Northern Ireland.

Then, I took a stint as an au pair in Germany outside of Cologne.

Part II

July 25, 1981

Dear Virginia!

Hi! I got your good letter yesterday and Boy – did it make my day a whole lot brighter! I've been pretty down lately mainly because of my own attitude and selfishness. The rainy weather sure doesn't help. I've been having a hard time feeling at peace here this past week. I'm tired much of the time and have not enjoyed work like I should. It's funny because sometimes I feel I am just over- qualified for this job now. Anyway, my thoughts keep focused on the future, and when I am not here. In the meantime, I have to learn to enjoy each day as it is and not be so tense. I feel that I have to be so perfect all the time because Hans, my boss, is really smart and I think he expects me to be too. Anyway, I have been very careless lately, and that has really been bothering me. I often wonder if I will always be so careless. Virginia, please excuse me for starting this letter like this! Your letter really brightened my day, and I thank you for it.

I don't think that I can get to Cologne in the beginning of August. I am making 500 DM (Deutsch Marks) for the whole summer. I automatically thought that 500 DM was about $1,000. I was very surprised when I got here to learn that it was not even $200! I need 400 for the Eurail Pass. I do have some extra money, but I am using it up in letters (thus the new postcards!). I will need some money to travel. So, I am working until the end of August. I will hopefully be done on Thursday, the 28th. I will work that day, and hopefully, afterwards, go to Austria to buy the Eurail Pass. If I purchase it here in Germany, I cannot travel here for free. Austria is pretty close, so I will go there to get it and change some money there. Then I will get the train to Cologne on Friday, August 29th. I will either get there the same day, or on Saturday, the 30th. I could then see you! I will probably be there 2 to 3 days until September 1st, I think. I know you have to go too. Would this set-up work out? My phone number is08144/256. I would really like to call you, but my financial story is not successful. You do not have to call me if you don't want to. I know it is expensive. But please tell me if my plans sound okay to you – thanks.

Grafrath – Bavaria, Germany

Don't worry about me Virginia. Lately, I have been getting along with the family. It was my own darn fault that I felt paranoid. I was afraid that I did not fit in. But all along, they never thought that at all. I am finally adjusting. It figures, it takes two months to adjust and that leaves me with only one month left to enjoy it. Your good letters and candy! Really made me smile. You are so special!

Yes, I heard from Diane B. She told me that Kent and Tracy will be getting married. They will make a super couple. Sometimes, I wish that I would settle down and find the right woman. But I will be in Tanzania for the next three years. Did I tell you? I will tell you all about it in Koln. I look forward to meeting your family there. Your host Dad sounds great. Oh, I have a beard if you can picture that!

Your situation sounds physically and emotionally draining as well. I am sure you are learning an awful lot from it. I know I am learning a lot myself by being here. The family does not sound like a very close one.

Oh yeah, thank you for those great chocolate wrappers! They were very beautiful and quite delicious! But I must admit, they were a little hard to swallow! Yes, I also got your great conehead post card. I was very impressed at how delicate coneheads can be!!! (I had sent Mark a post card with a picture of a lady from Bretagne on it. She was wearing the traditional dress and a very tall coronet head covering – resembling a cone.) I was actually relieved to get your postcard because I was not sure if you received my letter that I had sent to Ticonderoga. So, I sent another one to your address in Cologne with the help of Super Christy Wade! Christy is still going to school and she will graduate with a Soil Science Degree. She is working this summer in a health spa. Sounds like a lot of fun. I must say that she will be in the best of health, but she always was!

Your letter was super! You are so creative. I am in a good mood now because my host father gave me a raise of 500 DM. I thought it was 500 DM for the whole summer, but that is per month!

After this time in Grafrath, I will spend September in Europe. I sent a note to Pat Murphy. Do you think that she would mind me coming to her house? I know you were there and that you would like to see her again. I have written a few times from the states and have not heard a word from her. How is her home situation? I mean, I don't want to impose on them. I know there is a hunger strike going on there and a lot of political upheaval.

I am running out of room Virginia. I am so glad that you are here in Germany. I do hope that we can get together. Everyone at home is fine. I am glad to hear that your family is well too. I will be hearing from you then?

Love always,

Mark

In bold letters in the middle of this letter is cut-out of the words: **A Tradition of Friendship**

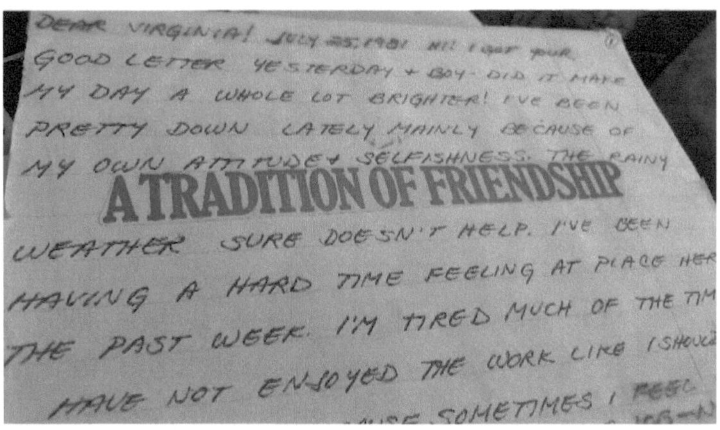

DEAR VIRGINIA! JULY 25, 1981 HI! I GOT YOUR
GOOD LETTER YESTERDAY + BOY- DID IT MAKE
MY DAY A WHOLE LOT BRIGHTER! I'VE BEEN
PRETTY DOWN LATELY MAINLY BECAUSE OF
MY OWN ATTITUDE + SELFISHNESS. THE RAINY
A TRADITION OF FRIENDSHIP
WEATHER SURE DOESN'T HELP. I'VE BEEN
HAVING A HARD TIME FEELING AT PLACE HER
THE PAST WEEK. I'M TIRED MUCH OF THE TIM
HAVE NOT ENJOYED THE WORK LIKE I SHOU
SOMETIMES I FEEL

August 13th

A Warm Beautiful Evening

Dear Virginia,

Sorry, this is a normal letter, but the post man scolded me, and my host mom also scolded me because my mail is too heavy. He said that it would have to be thinner, or he would have to charge me it as a letter. Little did he know! So, it is back to basics and away form creative engineering until I can come up with a way to seal the post-a-letter cards better so that they hold helium. Then I would not even have to pay a cent for a stamp! I could just let go of it and point it in your direction. If you think of any ideas, let me know!

I got your most recent carta yesterday, getting you in shape for Espana! You sounded as wonderful as ever. The third or fourth sounds fine Virginia, but I have other plans before that. So, if your Yugoslavian friends would not mind housing up a total stranger, that would be fantastic. Do you think they would mind? Otherwise, I could surely find something else to do. My plans are still very uncertain at this point. I have plans at this point to see Mike Schraeder and then I have a friend from my hometown who is in Norway, there is a friend in France, then a Spanish host family, and then maybe Patricia. I wrote to all the UWP folk a month ago – Ida, Bernie, Patricia, Janice – who did I forget? I asked them to write and to let me know if it was okay to visit. I have not heard from anyone except YOU of course! And Mike. I don't have much more time left to decide what I am doing. I am a bit paranoid to just pop in at UWP homes now. I feel if they wanted me to come, they would have responded. I feel that if anyone wrote to me in Connecticut, I would loved to have welcomed them there. I am not home much. Maybe it is the same for the Europeans. I just hope it isn't my personality! I am thinking that I may pop in on Patricia anyway because she may not have received my letter yet. Thank you for sending me her new address. I will write to her at once. I would really like to see her so much! She is so sweet with a tang of that Irish Celt - Mmmm!

I need to leave from your house and go straight to France because my friend said that between the fourth and tenth would be best. I would love more than anything to accompany you to Spain, but you see, it is not possible. I would love more than anything to see host families in Spain. But like a dummy, I did not plan to travel at all, and I neglected to bring those addresses with me. I am definitely going to write to my folks to have them send them to me. I needed to wait to hear of a job that I had applied to before I left. It wasn't until July that I knew for sure of a job acceptance which begins in November. So, I have only a month before that. Now I am thinking of just traveling for three weeks rather and waste, (me, waste?) a week of the Eurail Pass to get home earlier.

(*There is a watermelon spot on the letter. Quick, get the 'Whisk'! Mark writes.*)

I didn't want to tell you until I saw you, but you will see how it all fits Virginia. I will be doing some missionary work with a Mennonite group in Tanzania for three years. I feel that a month is not enough time to get all the required shots, get my eyes, medical and teeth checked as well as see friends and family before departing.

(Back to watermelon stain – or maybe I need "Spray 'n Wash"!)

I am also toying with the idea of seeing my sister in Arkansas before I go. So that extra week would come in handy. It will cost big bucks but the last time I saw my sister was during our summer break in UWP. Another three years would just be too long. That's if I can afford it, but with my raise, and if I really scrimp, it might be a possibility.

I also have friends from school (UCONN) and Massachusetts, but I will have to hitch hike to see them. That takes time, but luckily no money. I may even hitch hike to Pennsylvania for mission training. That is only a small maybe. I can't believe how cheap I am, not to mention poor. I know you can relate though. So, you can see how wishy washy it all is. One thing is certain, I will see you until the sixth when we must bid farewell.

Try and write about your Yugoslavian friends. I would love to learn more about Yugoslavia. It sounds fascinating and your friends sound so nice.

I am not sure how I am getting around yet. Foreigners who buy the Eurail Pass in Germany must purchase the 4-week one. If I travel in Germany, I will have to pay half the ticket cost. If I can get the ticket in Austria, it would be much less to get to you, and also to get to my plane. I have to look into all of this when I get to Munich. Everything is so confusing. You mentioned an Inter-Rail Pass – I don't know if this is the same as a Eurail train pass. I am assuming it is. How do you know how much it cost in Irish pounds? Are you planning to go to

Ireland to buy it? Maybe you checked it out at Patricia's.

Oh my gosh! You cannot believe this! Actually, I can't! At this very second that I am writing to you, babies are being born. I am sitting here at the kitchen table writing to you with this cute cat right next to me. I was scratching her belly, and all of a sudden, she starts screaming! I thought, "Oh no, Rabies!" Then suddenly, this black blob starts coming out! It turned out to be a cute kitten. I mean, Virginia, this very second, when I was in the middle of writing the word 'out' in the previous paragraph, it happened so fast. I knew she was on the heavy side, but really! I have never been a mid-wife before. Gol, it was a cinch. All I did was jump out of the way and told her to calm down. They just popped out, "Snap!" – like that. And most thought I knew nothin' bout birthin' babies! Maybe that qualifies me for a veterinarian certificate or something. Surely, I'll have to get paid for my services. My heart is still spastic!

So, I think business is taken care of as far as traveling and baby birthing goes.

So, Virginia, we'll both be sarcastic about it. I too am avoiding the word – Ugh! "Flexible", and we will get together real soon. Do not regret the change and try not to feel exploited. It's only a few more days. A 15 Million Dollar deal is much more important than a Million Dollar friend (O.K., O.K., so I am a 63-cent type of guy!) Herr Oehr sounds real nice.

No Virginia, that was the first time you used the stationary. I liked it. It is exactly two times the size of a post card. Maybe if you fold it in half, you can figure out a way to get that helium into it. The fudge spots smelled great. You really should have sent me a glass of it! What a blast when you said you made fudge. I thought it was that very faint yellow that is all over it. Maybe I am crazy, but I distinctly see it under lightbulb light. It is almost impossible to see it, but under sunlight, I swear I see a yellow design of some kind. I thought it was from your fudge, but I noticed it was the same on both sheets. Who knows. Maybe I am nuts. Speaking of nuts, did your fudge have nuts in them? Sounds yummy!

This week for me has been nice and peaceful. My boss and his wife are away on vacation. I am in charge, except for one of the boss's friends who comes in once a day to make sure the place didn't burn down. It's no big deal really. All I do is milk and feed the cows and spray weeds in the pasture. It's not like I am making up new feeding plans or harvesting grain all alone. It's just basic chores. It's a nice feeling to know he trusts me. Gol. It has taken me two and half months to adjust and now I will be leaving in two weeks. That seems to be normal.

The sixteen-year-old daughter is here too. We got along good at the beginning of the week. Now, I am not so sure. I think that we have a hard time communicating. I never know where she is at in terms of us getting along. She never asks me anything about me. I try to ask questions to just start conversation and then she laughs and says, “What a dumb question.” Okay, maybe it was a dumb question. I don’t know if she really thinks I am stupid or not. She is the type who chooses friends according to whether they are smart enough for her or not – not because of whether or not they are nice. Many of her acquaintances are so nice, but she does not like them because she finds them stupid. I don’t think she thinks I am stupid, but I sure would like to know exactly what is in her head. She is not very open with her feelings. Neither am I for that matter. I do think she wants me to stop acting “American”. Oh Virginia, I don’t mean to make a big deal out of this. I will work things out. Things always do. I will just have to stop trying to converse and being friendly. I will let her reach out, and then I will welcome it. Boy, I sure hope you can read this Virginia. I could talk forever. I am going to bed now. I want you to get this as soon as possible. I have to get up every day at 5 a.m. I can't wait for Hans to get back so I can sleep until 7 a.m. or something wild and crazy like that!

So, you get some rest too, even it if it 11:30 in the morning or whatever time you read this!

With love – God Bless You,

Mark

Because Mark loves cows, I often sent him the candy wrappers which happened to have a picture of a cow on it. I also sent him a chocolate bar on occasion.

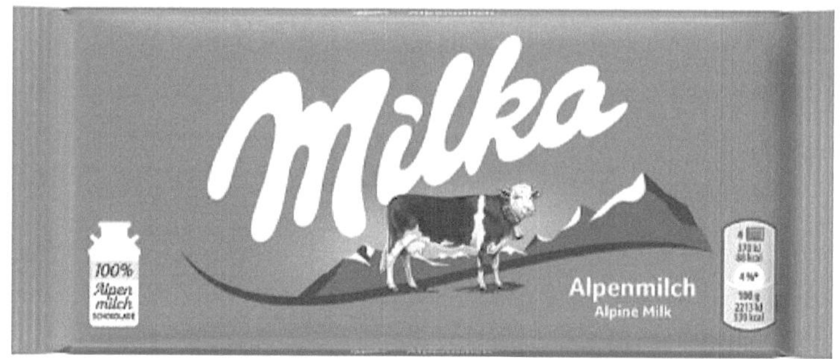

Dear Virginia,

WOW! That was the sweetest letter you every sent me and the sweetest I ever received! Those candy wrappers were great – especially the big one. I did not even have to put mustard on it. But it had some brown stuff inside. I did not know what it was, so I threw it away (only kidding!)

I also can't wait to see you! It has been nearly two years. It goes by so fast. I am sure you rare as you always were – warm and sincere!

Well, got to go. I hope you are in good spirits.

God Bless You!

Love always,

Mark

October 1981

Dear Virginia,

I am finally home and enjoying the fantastic October weather and foliage here in New England. It feels so good to be home. I don't know if I'll ever love Tanzania as I do here. I don't know where to send this, so I'm hoping your grandfather will forward it.

Mark and me – when he came to visit me in Germany

I do hope by now that you are on your trip and not working in Koln. You were there much longer than was good for your well being I think. I hope Mary can handle it. She is such a fantastic person, as was everyone. Do you know what Nervessa, Mensura, and Mensud did for me? I couldn't believe it! Frist, they gave me a lovely note full of good wishes. Then, they gave me 3 beautiful pictures of them. You were in one of them with Mensura – sitting on the car. They also gave me 20 DM and a beautiful pullover sweater. I just cannot get over how generous that family is. They are such beautiful people. To think they had to flee from war-torn Bosnia. I only wish that we had more time together. I did not deserve their overwhelming generosity. You were blessed by having them living there beside you.

Virginia, I had the best time in Koln visiting you. I know you felt bad because there was not more time off to spend it together alone. But I was not put out one bit. I loved Guillaume and Frederick. I did not mind Madame much. It was just fantastic and so relaxing just to be able to be lazy. It was also a blast getting into the city. I think the three of us had the best day ever. And thank you Virginia, for buying me that diary notebook. I am going to save it for when I am in Tanzania. I must admit, I like your taste in gifts!

So, you must be in Spain enjoying the sun, the people, and the fun. I do hope that it is as rewarding as you expected. I am sure it will be. I do hope you get to see Patricia. She's such a special person and I miss her terribly.

Virginia do write and tell me how you are. I will keep in touch in Tanzania. We will get together afterwards, Ok?

God be with you my friend,

Love always,

Mark

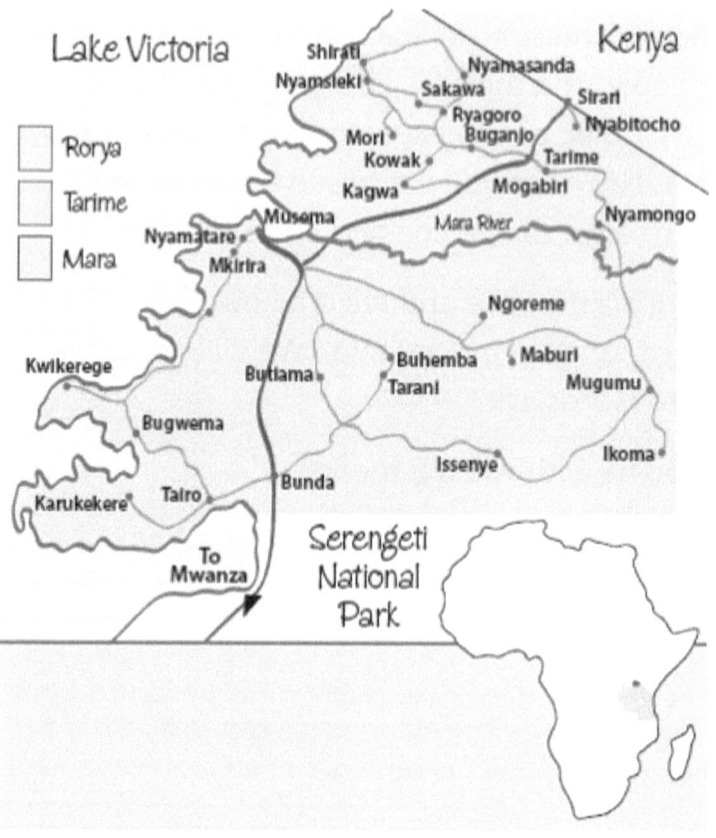

Lake Victoria
Kenya
Rorya
Tarime
Mara
Shirati
Nyamasanda
Nyamsieki
Sakawa
Sirari
Ryagoro
Nyabitocho
Buganjo
Mori
Kowak
Tarime
Kagwa
Mogabiri
Nyamongo
Musoma
Mara River
Nyamatare
Mkirira
Ngoreme
Kwikerege
Buhemba
Maburi
Butiama
Tarani
Mugumu
Bugwema
Ikoma
Issenye
Bunda
Karukekere
Tairo
To
Mwanza
Serengeti
National
Park

Part III

A Call to Serve

Mark had a strong desire to put his Christian faith into practice. This led him to the Mennonite Central Committee which sent him to Tanzania. Always faithful to his United Church of Christ heritage, he asked for and received appointment as an Associate Missionary.

Before Mark embarked on this project, he came to visit me while I was in Germany. My sister Mary was with me as she was going to resume my post with the family whose children I was caring for. Mark had gone for training in Switzerland. He came to us with his backpack, and he gave the family who we were staying with a box of walnut shaped cookies filled with a praline center. They came from the Black Forest. I think they were given to Mark, but he presented them as a gift to his host. They were delicious!

I thank You Lord with all my heart,

I sing praise to Your Name, Most High.

Ps. 9:1-2

Herein, are some edited excerpts from letters that Mark had sent to his Pastor, Reverend Luther C. Pierce of the Congregational Church in Monroe, Connecticut. These are interspersed with letters that mark sent to me.

January 1, 1982

I received many Christmas greeting from you all and I cannot tell you how much of an impact that has on my ability to endure in a new culture. THANK YOU!

I do not want to lose my United Church of Christ identity. Send me some information on Congregational history and the formation of the UCC. The Mennonites are much aware of their past. I find myself ashamed of my ignorance when they ask me questions about my church – both in the past and in the present. I know the Congregationalists sent out the first American missionaries, but I couldn't answer when someone asked the simple question, "Where?"

I have had some bit of a culture shock up to now. I think it has been due to adjustment to new values and coming to better understand my own shortcomings. I have felt a bit frustrated here at Buhemba by the fact that I am not working on a specific project yet. It has taken me up until now to realize that I need to learn patience. The ability to be patient and enjoy each new experience is important at this point.

January 23, 1982 from Buhemba

The war with Uganda has brought on shortages of commodities and heavy inflation. Although Tanzania won the war, they lost in a different way. I think the U.S. owes Tanzania much credit because it is this state that has paid for Amin's decline. The U.S. has benefited greatly at the expense of the Tanzanian economy. Actually, the whole world has.

Although there are many problems to be solved here, there are just as many to be solved at home. I am learning that it is not the place nor the amount of wealth a country has that creates problems. It is the imperfections of human beings that create injustice and suffering. It is selfishness, dishonesty, hate and impurity that causes it. Suffering is all over the world. The U.S. needs help as much as Tanzania does, just in a different way.

February 24, 1982 from Nairobi

I was surprised to find that the people in the UCC give only $166.45 per member outside the local church (14%) while the Mennonites give $404.00 per member (38%). I wonder how one group can be so generous. Of the 86% of the money that the UCC does not give to outside missions, what happens to it?

I was surprised that the U.S. has cut back by 70% food aid grants (BFW), and food aid loans by one third. I guess all we can do is pray and have hope. Would it be too much to ask the congregation to write to our representatives and senators? I know firsthand that Tanzania is in great need of immediate food and assistance.

February 27, 1982

Dear Virginia!

I figured it was about time that I sat myself down and wrote you a letter. I hope this finds you doing well. You must be back in New York by now and enjoying (?) the cold weather!

How is your family doing – especially your grandfather? Please say hi for me. How about Mary? How is she enjoying, or not enjoying, Germany and the Oehrs? I hope to write to both Mary and the Oehrs sometime. Have you heard from Arvid? He is a really nice person.

Well, Tanzania is a lot as I thought it was going to be, but it is really nice. It is not as humid as in the states, so I can enjoy the heat. It is a lot more beautiful than I imagined it would be. There is a lot of green here, and it is really hilly. Yup, everyone lives in mud huts here with grass roofs. It's neat. I have just a small normal (modest) house. It has only two hours of electricity a day and no fridge. There is no hot water and there is an outhouse. What more can a person want?

The Tanzanian people are really super. They love to laugh a lot. They are also fascinated by White folks which makes me a superstar just because I happened to be that way.

Right now, I am in language school. I am trying to master Swahili. They tell me that it is the easiest language in the world to learn. Somehow, I think that English is easier.

It is a real nice school. I have my room on the second floor. I even have a balcony that overlooks Lake Victoria which is the second largest lake in the world. It is really a super view.

All the teaching classes are done in Swahili and we have eight hours of classes a day. Then, we are expected to do another two to three hours in the Language Lab listening to tapes in Swahili. A lot of the time, I bring in some tapes of music to listen to instead. People think I study real hard... only if they knew!

I will be working at Buhemba Rural Aid Center on a dairy project when I get out of school. The World Bank was going to sponsor it, but that never materialized. So hopefully the government will be able to help us. The budget will have to be a lot smaller – 400,000 schillings as opposed to the original 3 million that was planned. Each schilling is equivalent to 12 cents. I think that it is better that way. It is better to start small and work up rather than start big and flop. We will be buying local heifers to breed with the Holstein bulls of Buhemba. We will then sell the pregnant heifers to the local farmers. Hopefully, this will increase production. One of the problems with that is the fact that the farmers like the prestige of owning cattle rather than the production that it can bring. It is like owning a car in the states. The more cattle one has, the richer he is. Cattle is like money. When a man wants to get married, he must pay the bride's father in cows!

Even though we are on the edge of Lake Victoria, we cannot go swimming in it. If we go, we are susceptible to getting a disease known as "Shisto". They tell us that we can go in as long as we swim 20 meters offshore. The problem is getting to that 20- meter mark. It is only localized. Eventually, I will be able to go swimming in other areas of the lake.

It is also easy to contract Malaria here. I have had it three times already. I must sleep under a net to keep the mosquitoes away at night. I also must take a Malaria pill once a week to prevent it. Of course, it does not always work. They say that it is not so bad if one does get the disease.

Well, Virginia, I better be going. I just wanted to tell you that I am thinking of you and I hope that you are well. Write when you get a chance. I often wonder how you are. I pray for your safety.

Love always,

Mark

March 28, 1982 from Nairobi (after a break in which Mark went back to Buhemba)

I must admit that before going to language school, one of the biggest frustrations was the fact that I could not really become good friends with the Tanzanians because we did not speak the same language. I felt that they were impressed with my improvement when I returned. They wanted to get to know me better as I did them.

April 20, 1982 from Nairobi

It is late at night and the boys of the local seminary next door are practicing for Sunday service tomorrow. I can hear the beat of the music; the drum pounding and keeping the pace of the singing. This is a nice preview for the next day. They often sing just before going to bed. It is very relaxing to listen to.

24 April 1982

My Dear and Special Good Friend Virginia,

Well, I just received your letter of March 21st yesterday. I was anxious to respond as soon as possible.

Thank you so much Virginia for your beautiful card and those super pictures. Why is it that you bring so much joy and happiness into people's hearts? Perhaps it is because of your great sincerity for what is right and of being of service to people. You are a very important person on this earth. I know that God has a very, very unique place for you in His Heart as I too have.

I have thought of you a lot lately because I have just received a beautiful card from Patricia. I was so happy that you two were able to get together. I only wish that I could have been there with you. I never did find out exactly what she was doing in NYC or in Kansas City. Maybe you can fill me in.

I have been thinking of writing to the Oehr's and to the Osmanagics. My pictures and addresses are back in the states. Maybe you can help me fill in the gaps with names and so forth. My memory is terrible. I do hope that they all got my thank you notes. I had such a fantastic time there with you and Mary.

The world is full of God's people.

Thank you for sharing your feelings with me. I know God has a plan for me here. Love really makes a person's emotions so intense and real at how much you travel.

How was your trip to California? It must have been beautiful out there. Did you see any of our UWP folk from that area? That reminds me, guess who getting married. Miss Christy Wade! Yup! I think she graduates this May. Boy, time sure does change.

I think you would really like it here Virginia. The Tanzanian people are such beautiful people. I am constantly amazed by their whole way of life. Even though they are one of the poorest people around, they are one of the most generous. If one person goes hungry, they share their food and resources. Everyone is on the same level. They love to laugh, and to sing and to dance. They pray most beautifully, often singing their prayers. Our attitude of life as Westerners is often viewed as a set of problems to be solved, to be conquered. The Tanzanians view life as a mystery to be explored. Every experience is an adventure. How haughty I have been to think that I had come to teach the Tanzanians what is right. I am finding that I have so much more to learn! I have been humbled by living here.

I am still in Language School and can see the end. It is almost over, June 2nd. I look forward to getting out and using what I have learned. I am getting tired of the routine of class for eight hours a day. One thing that does help, is the fact that we have a really good group. There are only twenty of us here. We have grown very close. Most of the people are priests and religious Sisters. They offer so much. Being here has opened my eyes to the Catholic

Church. I have really learned to value and appreciate the ways of the Catholic Church. It is remarkable and it offers so much. I am one of the youngest people in the class. They all think that I am a "nice boy". Oh well, someday, I will be considered otherwise.

Anyway Virginia, I better be going. I will be praying for you in your new experiences. I know they will all add up to make one remarkable book. I know you will get it written. I can only support you in word and prayer. Do take care of yourself Virginia. I pray that God takes care of you as you explore the mystery of life. Do write soon.

Love always,

Mark

13 May 1982

Dear Virginia,

Hello to my very special friend Virginia! How are you? I hope that this letter finds you in God's Grace. I hope you can forgive me for writing to you so late. I have been busy with the end of school and moving back to Buhemba. The time here just flies, but I guess that it does not fly any faster than it ever has! Maybe I am getting old and senile and just don't know where the time is going! Well, anyway, forgive me.

You are amazing Miss M. Virginia LaPointe! Now don't tell me you are thinking of going off and becoming a Maryknoll missionary! Well, if that is what the Lord wants for you, I am very excited. Surely, you would be wonderful in serving the Lord overseas. You are perfect for it, with all your experiences. Not only that, but you have such a sincere and pure Faith. I think that no matter what He has in store for you, you would be able to serve Him well. I got to know some of the Maryknollers here pretty well. I am very impressed with them! They are well-known for their emphasis on knowing the language well before beginning their work. Their language training is excellent. They study here for 4 months in Tanzania and then they have another two months of language practice. They choose a mission to go to just to practice the language and to get to know and understand the culture. My own language practice equals work. The Maryknollers realize that it is vital to have a good grasp on the language. They have people working in all areas. I am very impressed with them. Some work on large elaborate projects while others work in the village and work directly with the people. The participant really has a lot to choose from depending on what type of lifestyle they want to live in.

I was also very moved on what I have come to learn about the Catholic Church. I understand that great strides have been made since the

Second Vatican Council and that this has been kind of a reformation for the Church. There may have been a period of questioning in the sixties, but they have so much to offer us Protestants. In fact, I think they have passed us in keeping up with modern Theology. It is really exciting for me.

Thank you so much for filling me in on everyone in Germany. I have been wanting to write to them for a long time, but I forgot a lot. I have the pictures of you and Mary and Guillaume up. I really thank you for the pictures. I will always be reminded of my fantastic stay in Koln. I really admire you and Mary. It is comforting to know that if I can't find a job in farming when I return in 1984, I can get a job there taking care of the kids. I cannot control kids at all. They would get away with murder with me. If they got a few cows, I would consider it though.

I have been adjusting fast to my place here at Buhemba. I really love it here. I have been spending a lot of time just orientating myself and getting the house in order. I have been cooking for myself. I find it hard because I am not suer how much to buy without a fridge. Things spoil so fast here. I bought some meat yesterday and today it has already starting to go bad. I just finished cooking it for tomorrow. I hope it will help – who knows.

I got a chance to visit a Mennonite hospital. I had to get a vaccination. Anyway, I took the bus on the way back. It was quite an experience, but also a lot of fun. I was ready to get the 7:30 a.m. bus at the stop. In fact, I got there at 6:30 a.m. It did not come until 10:00. They had a flat or something. Because it was close to the Kenyan border, the police made everyone get out. Everyone's bags were checked for black market. We did not get going until 10:30. The bus was so crowded that I had to stand. Then we stopped again because we got another flat. They worked on three tires. It was four in the afternoon. We were supposed to have arrived at one o'clock. Then, we had to get out two more times at police checks. We got to town at 8:30 p.m. – only seven and a half hours late! I had to stand most of the way like others. After a while, some Tanzanians gave me their seat. They were so friendly. I enjoyed them a lot. I like to travel the way they have to. It helps me understand the people better.

Well, I can see that I am running out of room. I have been doing well with cooking, the Swahili, my garden, etc. I pray for you Virginia. Please let me know what you are doing this summer. Do say hi to your Grandpa. Thanks Virginia. You are super. Take care and God Bless,

Love,

Mark

May 25, 1982 from Nairobi

I have been reading 'Beyond Ujamaa' by Goran Hyden. It is one of the first books by an African that critically analyzes Africa, specifically Tanzania. Hyden claims that most of the people are living on a subsistence level and are not very dependent on the government. This means that people often feel no need to change their lifestyles in spite of government policies that urge change. He refers to the public as "organic" as opposed to "inorganic" of the developed countries. Organic peasants get most of their needs from the farming they do at home. To industrialize Tanzania, the government must first "capture" the peasants so that the public do those things which will help the country develop. I am not sure that most people want to develop a Western style. Traditions here are very strong. Development is a long process that cannot be done in a matter of thirty years.

The missionary field is an exciting field to be in at this time. We are being humbled as servants and have as much to learn from the people here as they have from us.

June 26, 1982 from Buhemba

I've come to the conclusion that development cannot be equated with "Westernization" because the cultures vastly differ. Traditions are very important and most people here value their past. Often the authorities promote a Western idea of development, but their efforts fail because the majority of people do not want it. There seems to be a big gap between what the government wants and what the people want.

August 1, 1982 from Buhemba, following the attempted coup in Kenya

Personally, I feel that Kenya is heading in the direction of many of the countries in Central America. Much of the land is owned by a few people. The rich are getting richer. There is more oppression of those who speak against the government. The military seem to be more involved in political affairs. Time will tell what will eventually happen.

.

Mark in Africa – *He had looks thinner than before he left. He also sent me a picture of him with a coconut on his head. He has such a great sense of humor.*

15 August 1982

Dear Virginia!

It was so good to hear from you. Your letters really make me feel so good. I am always happy to hear that you are doing well.

But first of all, I want to both scold you and thank you for that "Tidbit" as you called it. Now M. Virginia LaPointe, you should not be so generous and thoughtful! That is not just a tidbit, but a whole lot of money! Thank you, Virginia a thousand times over and then some. I am including a little tidbit of my own. I know it won't be helpful, but it will be interesting. Believe me, it is not very much, but you inspired me to share my own wealth. The interesting thing about Tanzanian money is that when you hold it to the light, and look to the left of

President Nyerere, what do you see? Right! There should also be a line going down somewhere in the middle. We call it magic money. It is not worth much more than play money.

I was so happy to hear that you are doing well. By now, your sister Mary has probably returned from Germany. I hope that she had a good time. Please tell her I said howdy. Now she can be content at home and take in all that she has learned.

I appreciate your trust in me. Know that you are in my constant prayers.

It was nice if bittersweet to hear from an old friend. Christ really makes people more alive, and a person can put out 110%. The Lord is amazing, perhaps too much so for many people.

Anyway, life at the farm has been good. The Lord is present. I have relied on Him a lot lately. At times I need someone to confide in and get advice. He is so easy to confide in and get advice. However, a lot of the time it is not the advice that I want to follow. He knows what is best.

I have been real busy. I've been patiently waiting for the money to be available to start this project. It is hard to believe that I have been here almost ten months and have yet to get into the work that I was assigned. Things like this take a long time in a Third World country. A person can go nuts if he wants or does not want! I am working now on a small tree nursery to help increase the supply of lumber and firewood. A lot of that stuff is being depleted due to the fact of fuel costs being so high. The forests are being depleted which can lead to desertification. It is a pretty serious problem in the Third World. This is only a very small project. I doubt it will have much impact on a large scale. Hopefully, it will do some good. I feel that too often large projects become so big that they leave the local people out of the plan with very little benefit.

Actually, I am going through a period of uncertainty at this point. Many missionaries go through a low period between the 8th and 12th month. I am finding it hard living alone, and not finding very many people to speak English to. I go to bed exhausted after trying to express myself all day. Also, I can't help but wonder if people are nice to me to get something, or just to be friends. I am learning so much about other people, the mission movement, and about the world especially Africa. It is really an exciting place to be.

Well Virginia, I better be going. Please say hi to Mary for me. Congratulate her on spending a whole year in Germany! Also, give your grandfather my warmest regards. I know you are taking good care of each other. I thank God for that. So, do take care of yourself, Virginia, as well as others.

God Bless you my dear good friend,

Love,

Mark

October 1, 1982 from Buhemba

I see the need for a real revival of spirituality all over the world. Even here in Tanzania. There is a need for people to put Jesus at the center of life. It is true that when He becomes the center of our lives, that life in the Church and at home become more meaningful. We all need periods of renewal in our lives, including myself. Actually, I need a period of renewal every day, whether it be in quiet time or whether I am working alone. God speaks in all kinds of circumstances.

Life here is going well. I have gone through a period of self-evaluation and an evaluation of the Tanzanians. It was a long period of culture shock. I felt that everyone was coming to me to bother me about selling things or giving them away. I have finally come to grips with it and realize that I cannot supply all the watches, cameras and radios wanted of me. I have found that as I get to know people better, they stop asking for all kinds of things and as a result, we get to know each other on a more personal level.

November 2, 1982 from Buhemba

I am continually adjusting to Tanzania. I still have difficulty dealing with the great difference in lifestyle between the missionaries and the people we are here to serve. I am definitely living very simply compared to the standards of the U.S. Yet, I live at a level here that is unimaginable to most Tanzanians. For example, I spend about ten times more per month than what a Tanzanian makes. I don't think that I will ever feel comfortable with the difference.

Friends are not only together
when they are side-by-side
even one who is far away...
is still in our thoughts.

Mark was very artistic. He made the card with an enclosed letter – on previous page. He took the time to burn the edges for effect.

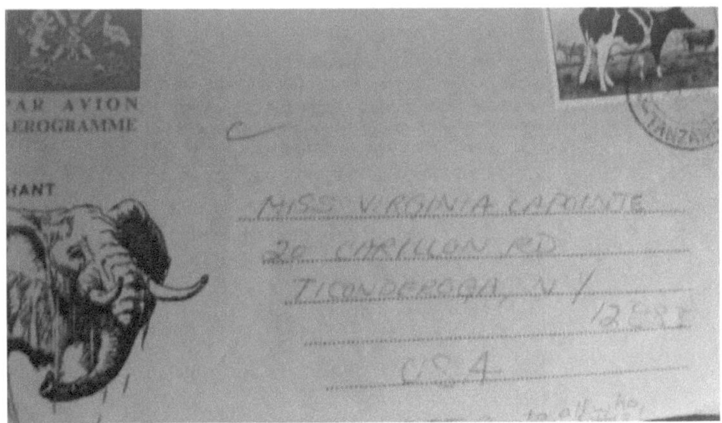

November 8, 1982

Dear Virginia,

It is exactly two months since you wrote your letter and a month since I have received it. Will you ever forgive me for my procrastination? I have been thinking about you a lot lately, but I seem to get farther and farther behind in my letter writing. Continually, I am feeling guilty about it. "Hiccup – just got them – hic".

I was so happy to receive your last letter. You are such a warm and sincere person. God bless you. I do hope that this letter finds you in good health and spirits.

I often think about our UWP year, 1979, and what my blessings are that were produced from that experience. There are a few who are top quality. Thank you for being one of those blessings.

You mentioned in your last letter that Mary is back home. How is she doing? Please say hello to her for me. You know, I keep thinking of that family. It breaks my heart for the stepson. He needs love so badly. Boarding school is not the answer. I think the whole family could benefit with some real help – spiritual. I wish they could know the Lord Jesus Christ as a family. I think their excess wealth blinds them to so much of real life. I would love to help them. I would gladly work for them for a year, but it would have to include the stepson in addition to the other children in order for me to do it. Anyway, I have another service to fulfill. I must not work for someone out of pity with the expectation of sharing my faith. I have never been very good about testifying my faith. I feel a failure in this respect. It is goal that I hope to reach – to be more open and evangelistic without being overbearing. I just wish that those without faith could feel what I feel. I never see any effect of my ministry. I should not expect quick results. I am too demanding on that.

Speaking of faith. It has occurred to me that it is necessary for me to marry a Christian. It is a priority. I believe that it is a rare occurrence for a Christian and a non-Christian to have a good marriage. I need someone with the same basic values. Christianity is about as basic as one can get.

Anyway, I admire your strength and character Virginia. Are you still minding the elderly woman? Does she live in your town? Please say hi to your grandfather for me. He is a very special person with such unconditional love for you. I guess it is mutual.

Well, that didn't leave me much room to expound on what's happening here. That's okay because there really isn't a lot. I have already had my first -year anniversary with the Mennonites. Soon, will be my first -year anniversary with the Tanzanians (Nov. 16th). No one knows about my big anniversary. I doubt anyone would care. It is a good time to reflect. I have to sit down and get some concrete thoughts written! So, don't ask me what has happened in the year. The time went by like it was a day. It has been really hard at times, but always worthwhile. Sometimes, I feel awful paranoid and incompetent, but I have plenty of time to adjust and learn.

We are finally getting started with the crossbreeding project! I can't believe it! I thought it would never happen. I feel like a whole year has gone by wasted. But reality, I learned a lot. Today we measured out the area to be cleared of brush and trees. We picked out two bulls to be used. Actually, I think that if I was not here, that they would do just as good a job. There is just a lot of people doing nothing.

Anyway, I feel pretty happy and hopeful for the future.

The tree project is going well. However, a cow got into the area. Thank God, he only stepped on a few trees. We are beginning to sell them this week. So far, no takers. I am not too disillusioned as yet. I just put the notice up today! So, lately, I have been feeling good about my work here.

Well Virginia, let me end here (Do you have a choice?). Please remember that you are very special to me and always will be. I pray you

have a blessed Thanksgiving. Do take care of yourself. God Bless you.

God Bless you.

Love always,

Mark

P.S. – I'm real proud of my Dad. He was in the New York Times Sunday paper! August 15th, page 1 of one of the sections!

Part IV

Mark's 1982 Annual Report

This being my first year as a missionary, I arrived with a lot of idealism. One of the first things that hit me was the strong difference in the standards of living between the missionaries and the Tanzanians. It may be harder to find commodities here, but we still find and accumulate them. It must absolutely astound the Tanzanians to see all the junk we call necessities. Their sense of sharing and close community makes it hard for them to understand why we don't give more freely. Their asking and begging makes us defensive. As a result, we begin to build human barriers. We become cynical. We are here to give, and they want more and more. Perhaps this coveting is provoked by the inequality of lifestyles. It is important to be ever conscious of our wealth. It is easy to flaunt it without even knowing it. Being sensitive to this problem can prevent a defensive and cynical attitude.

The Tanzanians are not inhibited as we are. Their easy-going lifestyle is refreshing. Each person is a real individual. I am enjoying getting to know them.

This past year has been one of spiritual growth. Buhemba offers a slower paced lifestyle. The people are not bombarded by the sights and sounds of the mass media and advertising. There are no bowling alleys, no movies, no arcades to distract one. The quiet has provided me with time to meditate and to emphasize non-material pleasures. It is much easier to do without things when one can't get them. Hopefully, this attitude will stick with me when I return to the immense consumer society that is America.

January 5, 1983

I have just returned from a trip to Arusha having gone with a friend whose parents came out for a visit. It was quite a trip because we had to travel through the Serengeti National Park. The wildlife in it is amazing!

It was the time of the year when the rains were very heavy. The road was in terrible shape. We were fortunate to have a Land Rover with four-wheel drive. We would have been in a lot of trouble otherwise. We saw trucks and buses literally being pushed up mountains by people. These large vehicles left ruts two feet deep making it that much more difficult for smaller cars. There were some places where the road was completely under water. We had to drive long distances to avoid them. One detour took us to Shirati Hospital, the place where we had borrowed the vehicle. Since it was a 250-mile round trip to take me back to Buhemba with the Land Rover and would cost $70.00, we decided that I would take the bus back which cost only

$5.00. Unfortunately, there was no bus, and I ended up hitchhiking the whole way home.

Postmarked January 14, 1983

New Haven, Connecticut

Dear Virginia,

Have just received your fantastic letter yesterday. It is December 31st, 1982 and I am finally getting my Christmas cards written.

I want to thank you very much for your very good letter. You really are an inspiration.

Please forgive me for being so short with this. A friend is visiting from the states and is going home tomorrow. I want to send my cards back with her.

I was very happy to hear from you. How was your Christmas? How is your grandfather? Please tell him that I said hello.

I was very happy to hear of your plans to go to Ireland. Perhaps by the time you get this you will be back. Did you get to see Patricia? How is she?

Life goes on here. I am enjoying it tremendously. I finally feel that I can call this home without feeling like a foreigner. I am still learning so much about the world and God's people. There are so many problems, but the blessings overcome them. I am even a little nervous at this point thinking of my return. It is such a such a fast, visually and audibly-oriented society there. Here, the pleasures are much more simple but the need for Christian witness is far greater in the states. I am not sure that I want to come back to the states and live on a farm in Vermont like I have always dreamed. I am so confused about my future. I should not be so self-centered. I suppose everyone is a little apprehensive about his future one time or another.

Well, I best go. Thank you so much again for your beautiful letter. You are so special to me. Oh, I know those Maryknoll Sisters from Kgombe. Please have a GOOD 1983. I hope to hear from you soon.

Take care and God Bless,

Love,

Mark

Heri ya Sikukuu

Happy Christmas - (this is on the blue aerogramme)

Feb. 2, 1983

Dear Virginia!

Howdy! How are you! I am finally getting my back end and my right hand in gear and doing some letter writing. Actually, I am in a guesthouse. Most of them here, well, all of them, are Bordellos, but the room is affordable. And no, I do not partake in the extra services offered. Anyway, I am in the other side of the country waiting to get a plane back home (Buhemba). They keep canceling the planes. Air Tanzania is not known for its reliability. I will explain why I am here later.

Anyway, how are you? Boy, do I look forward to hearing from you! How was your trip? I am sure it was fulfilling for you. Did you get to see Patricia? I had a nice card and note from her. She sounds like she is doing well.

How is your grandfather? I hope he is doing well. Tell him I said hi.

So, you talked to Christy Lamb – Wow! I sure would like to see her again! She is so nice. I would love to hear from her. It does not seem possible that our UWP year was four years ago! Are we getting old or what? I have not heard from many folks. I did get a note from Joy Tucker – very thoughtful of her. Once in a while I hear from Larry Swenson which is very nice. I hear from Dianne now and again.

Anyway, let me know what you are doing, and how you are feeling, and what you are thinking. You are a precious friend and I really care for your person and spirit.

I must admit, I have been kind of busy. Please do not think I am popular, but I guess I must know some rich people. Over Christmas, I had a friend come over from the states. This past week, my Pastor came out for a visit. Boy, talk about getting spoiled! It has been great entertaining, but really, I am pretty homesick now. It is also a drag because I also have to go back to work now. Ugh!

My pastor couldn't come out to see me at Buhemba so I went here to Arusha to meet him. He came out with a group touring East Africa. We had a fantastic time. We had the opportunity to go to Lake Manydra, and the Ngorongoro Crater. We saw all kinds of fantastic animals: lions, elephants, giraffes, zebras, rhinos, hippos, etc., etc. Amazing! It was not all fun, because we got five flat tires in one day and two in the next! One of the flats cost US$75 to fix! Expensive place this Tanzania! They were only here a few days, and it went by very fast. We also got to visit some local churches which was very interesting.

As far as work goes, I really have not done a whole lot of it lately. I haven't been home. The project goes on slowly, but surely. I have the ideal job – there is no responsibility. It fits me perfectly because I really am irresponsible. We have got pasture cleared. Next, we will put up a fence. That's if we can find the materials!

Well Virginia, I better get going. I do hope this finds you doing well. Let me know how you are. Do take care, and God Bless.

Love always,

Mark

February 17, 1983 from Buhemba

I have been home for two weeks now after having gone to Arusha to with Pastor Pierce and his traveling seminar for three days. It was very exciting to have Pastor come out and visit. It is hard to believe how fast the time went by. I must admit that I have one of the most supportive churches in North America. THANKS!!!

(Pastor's note: I was a member of a Plowshares Institute traveling seminar that visited the

churches and people of Kenya, Uganda, and Tanzania under the direction of Dr. Robert Evans. Mark's presence with us for the three days we were in Central Tanzania added an element of "missionary presence" deeply appreciated by all of us. Seeing Mark in the field was a highlight of the trip for me.)

When I came home, one of a staff's member's children had passed away. We prepared for a funeral. All the men get together to dig the grave. Each is supposed to have at least one turn. One must remove one's shoes while digging the grave because it is not clean. This stems from the Muslim influence in the country. After the service, visitors are allowed to go to the family's house. Visitors will stay all day and the young girls will cook a meal at dinnertime. The men stay on all night and sleep right there. The family will have visitors for the next three days and three nights. People also usually give gifts such as money, sugar, flour or soap. It was interesting to learn the customs.

March 14th, 1983

Dear Virginia,

Your most charming letter came to me this past week. I can't tell you how good it was to hear from you Virginia. You are just something else! I loved hearing about your escapades. You sure live one exciting life! I am really happy to hear that you are well and happy and in the Lord's care. You are one very special friend. Your happy, carefree personality really makes people feel very cheerful. Thank you for being my friend.

I just love your exquisite taste in writing material. It is just like you to be so creative and sparkling. The best of both worlds: the international flavor of the Shannon International Hotel, put together with the warmth and hominess of Holly Hobbie gift paper. How marvelous!

Well, I must admit, your latest adventures sound most exciting. I was curious to know how your time in Ireland was. Things are very bad there as I understand it. I admire your courage to settle there and experience what most people are afraid of. You are a most strong-willed individual. I have no doubt that you will get your book written!

That reminds me of Patricia. Have you got her U.S. address? I sure would like to have it. I was disappointed that we were not able to get together before I left. I was pretty sure that she was in Brooklyn or something which is pretty close to where I live. If you hear from her, please let me know. I cannot imagine why she remains so aloof. Did I tell you that I received a card with a few words and no return address at Christmas? Anyway, I think of her often and I pray for her safety. I know life must be difficult for her.

I am also glad to know that you made it to Spain and that you had a fantastic time! The Spanish are such warm and giving people. I remember giving one of my Spanish host families a surprise. They were very, very happy to have me in their home and welcome me. I don't think that I could even dream of popping in someone's home in the states.

I am glad to hear that you are back in Ticonderoga and resting a bit. Perhaps before your next adventure, you can include Tanzania in your plans. Well, it is nice to dream.

The Levy's sound like interesting people. It must have been something to have met all those famous and rich people. I do hope you got their autographs! I would have loved to have visited you there, but I think that the excessiveness of their lifestyle would have been too much for me. This leaves me disconcerted with people. I think the best of people when I don't have to deal with them. Then when I do, it strengthens my own values. I am much happier to be the salt and potato type as you mentioned in your letter. I do think our lives are a bit more stable and a lot more fun, wouldn't you agree?

It is good to hear you are home where your heart lies. I know your grandfather is happy to have you near. He really thinks so much of you and worries like crazy when you are scampering about the world. Let me know of your plans. Did that jazz group work out?

Things on this side of the world do not compare with your stories. I think I wrote to you a few weeks ago. Please accept my apologies for any reoccurrence of old news. Not a heck of a lot happens here, not that I am complaining. I love it here and I enjoy the time that I have. God knows, it is a short life. Every second is worth living to the fullest.

Next week we have a ten-day vacation from Language School. I will need it. I have been studying very hard to grasp Swahili. It is not a hard language, but it is really important to be able to communicate. I feel like I am in college again. I am studying so much. I realize that at times I do not put enough time into it. It shows when I am socializing and being with people. There is a balance and slowly I am learning what balance is good for me.

I did get to do a real UWP (Up With People) type thing. Our school visited a local textile mill. I could not believe how "UWP-ly" it was. But it was still very interesting. I learned a lot. It was a little different than the one we saw in the South. I am not sure what city that was – maybe Goldsboro? Anyway, it was refreshing to know that attempts are being made to industrialize Tanzania. It was started by the French and someday, it will be taken over by the Tanzanians. Who knows when. The French live very close to the school. We got to know them pretty well. They let us go swimming in their pool when we want. Despite being close to Lake Victoria, we are unable to swim in it. I think I told you before about that disease called 'shisto', also called 'Bilharzia'. So, there is something to do.

I have started a garden here. It is just a small one. It has been a lot of work because the soil is not very good. I had to carry 25- wheel barrels of dirt from a different place. It is really a good feeling to be outside and working with the earth. I will leave by the time the garden is ready to harvest. I am sure that the next group of people will enjoy the fruits. It is just a nice excuse to get out and do something. Other than Swahili, I am excited because I only planted a week ago and the sun flowers are already coming up!

I also just recently went to a typical Tanzanian dance. It sure was a new experience. They sure can dance. They just go, go, go until they practically drop from exhaustion. They are also very loose and uninhibited. It is wild. I was surprised when a guy asked me to dance. Men often dance together as well as women with women and of course men with women. It was a lot of fun.

Well Virginia, I must leave the page, but I think of you often. I pray for your health and happiness. I know you are safe in The Lord's hands. I thank God for knowing you. I hope to hear from you soon. You are just someone real special.

Take care and God Bless,

With Love,

Mark

March 16th, 1983

Dear Virginia,

Thank you so much for your last letter and the clipping you included. Yes, I know Father Mike Snyder, the one in the picture of the Maryknoll Fathers. Those Maryknoll missionaries really get their pictures published. I know all of them that were in that article.

Thank you for sending me the letter of yours that was published. It was a beautiful article. If that is the style that you are going to write your book in, can I put my order in now?! Maybe I am too early, but don't sell them all before I get a copy – that is when it comes out! You were so lucky to be in such a beautiful place filled with the warmth of the people. I would love to visit Ireland and to see Patricia. Maybe someday.

I hope this letter finds you doing well. There is so much to be thankful for. I am constantly amazed at God's Creation. What is going through your head these days? Are you still working for the elderly lady? Thank you so much for that really beautiful letter Virginia. You really are a very sensitive and warm person.

I got a nice card from Mrs. Williams. I am ashamed because I have not answered it yet.

How is Ticonderoga? I would really love to visit it because I love history. So much can be learned from look back in the past. It is interesting because each generation tends to think that it is different from the past ones. We might wear different clothes and play with different toys, but we are no different. People go through the same problems and the same joys. We could really change if we learned from the past. Instead, we concentrate on the future, and make the same mistakes.

Hey, did I tell you that I read an article on what your beloved 'anchor' symbol means? It is very fitting for you as it depicts the Hope one has in Christ.

I am glad that you saw Patricia. I hope that she is happy. I want only the best for her as she is such a special person.

Are you attending the UWP five- year reunion? I get out in November of 1984. I won't be able to go. I am enjoying it here a lot despite the fact that I am 99 and 44% confused about my future. I am content, and I know that God will provide. I find my strength in the Lord. I am loving it here and have to be content in the present. I need time to plan for the future. OH, who knows what I am saying!

Well, Virginia, I am going to get going. Do take care and God Bless!

I love you always,

Mark

April 4, 1983 from Buhemba

The MCC boss from Nairobi came for a short visit. It only seemed right that I would do my best to impress him especially since he is a very intellectual person. Not being very intellectual myself, I was a little nervous at first on how I should act. Anyway, I put dinner in the pressure cooker. While it was cooking away, I decided to take a shower. As I got out of the shower, and was putting one leg in my pants, my foot got caught in a hole and at the same time, the lid of the pressure cooker blew off. Dinner was spraying all over the kitchen! I had to think fast, and of course ran through the house with only my underwear and pants caught on one foot to get the pressure cooker off the heat. Meanwhile, my boss is sitting there patiently wondering why the heck I am running around the house like a chicken without a head with only the bare essentials on! Finally, when it was all over, we both had a good laugh. Here I was, trying ever so hard to be real suave and cool and I come off acting really dumb. God really works in funny ways to help us out. He really is an amazing God!

April 25, 1983 from Buhemba

Tanzania is going through a rough time right now. It has become much poorer over the years. Thus, stability is at stake. There is a lot of tension because the government is not carrying out its promises. President Nyerere seems to be the stabilizing factor. When he finally retires, Tanzania will go even further down hill and become more chaotic. The police will try to keep a handle on the situation. The stronger they get, the more chaotic it will become. There is a fine line between a free society and a police state.

PAR AVION
KWA NDEGE
YOUNG WARTHOG
TANZANIA
14
MISS VIRGINIA M. LAPOINTE
20 CARILLON RD
TICONDEROGA, N.Y.
12883
USA

Dear Virginia,

I have been meaning to write for so long now. I am almost embarrassed to start now. I decided this maybe this card would help you realize that I do think of you and pray for you often. By the time you receive this, you will be wondering where the heck I am.

Way back in March, you thought that maybe I was on my way back home to the states! I assure you Virginia, that I am still in Tanzania. At this point, nothing can take me away from here – except if it is the end of my term! I really misled you. I was in the airport waiting for my Pastor to arrive from the States. We met in the airport here in Tanzania. We spent about five days together until he left for home. We sure had a good time.

One other thing I must do, is thank you so much for your Easter card, gift, and wish. It seems so long ago now. I guess it is. But please believe me Virginia, when I tell you that I am sincerely grateful for all you do for me. Your letters are a real blessing. I always feels so good inside when

I hear from you. Please don't lose touch. Our friendship is too special. I only wish I could do as much for you as you do for me. Thank you, Virginia for your gifts, your support, and just your down-to-earth self!

How are you, Virginia? Are you still working for the elderly lady? Please give your grandfather special greetings from me. Is Mary still in California? You mentioned that you were thinking of returning to college and going to China. Are these still your plans? I'd really like to know. You had very little about yourself in your last letter. I look forward to hearing about you!

I hope you are enjoying the Summer weather. I bet Ticonderoga is just beautiful right now. I get so homesick for some beautiful Northeastern weather and scenery that sometimes I could cry. Tanzania sure is beautiful, but you know there is no place like home. (Now, whoever said that!!!)

God is so close to us all, yet He gives us the concept of time as both a learning and healing tool. This astounds me.

Have you heard from the Osmanagics lately? Please tell them I said hello when you next write. I just fail in writing and yet I have wanted to write to them and give them warm greetings. I shall never forget their generosity to me. This world needs more people like them.

Well Virginia, I don't have very much to report about the life of any of the missionaries. It has been pretty quiet here, and I have been enjoying the relaxation of being home. I did go on a small weekend retreat recently. It was a nice time. I had not seen some of the people since Christmas. When I returned, I discovered that I had guests while I was away. They must have been very uncouth as they did not use the door. Rather, they climbed in the window! Once they were in, they must have assumed that the things that were lying around were there for the taking. They were rather conservative taking some soap and all of my American money. It surprised me because I had all kinds of things of value lying around. They left the house in a pretty careless state – with not so much as signing the guest book! Nor did they fix the broken window. So, I am a little poorer than I was a few weeks ago. It serves me right for being rich among the poor.

The project moves as slow as ever. Nonetheless, I find this snail's pace too fast. It is a very even and fair system. We, the missionaries at the Center, blame the government officials for the lack of progress while they blame us. We all make very good scape goats. We, at the Center, are still waiting to get the very important materials needed to start building. The responsibility of the government is to supply us with the materials.

Meanwhile, I just enjoy socializing and concentrate on the social aspect of being a missionary. I often don't feel very adequate in this role. I should spend more time with the

Tanzanians. But I do require a good amount of time alone.

Well Virginia, I have enjoyed this time with you immensely. I sure wish you were here to talk to face to face. Hey, will you be going to the UWP reunion? Personally, I think Tanzania is a more appropriate place for it to be held. It may be the worst place in the world for a convention, but it does have potential. At least the only place Tanzania can go is up. It cannot go any further down.

Oh Virginia, do take care, and God Bless you.

Love always,

Mark

May 31, 1983 from Buhemba

It would be greatly helpful if you could remember Africans in your prayers as they face coming hardships. Most African are peasant farmers and have no insurance against natural disasters. Also, pray for the donor organizations that hey might be able to distribute food aid effectively and to the right people. Often food aid is poured into places where it is not really needed causing catastrophic results to the local economy. At other times, food aid is sold at great profits en route to its destination. And, sometimes, a country is deluged with so much food, its transportation system cannot handle it. As a result, it rots at port. Pray for great wisdom for all those involved.

July 4, 1983 from Buhemba

I continue to enjoy meeting and talking with the people around me. Although the Tanzanians are very different than we are, and it takes some adjustment to get to know them, the people are very friendly and generous. It has taken some time to understand the Tanzanian perception of friendship. If one says that I am a friend, it can mean anything from someone who gives him something to someone he can talk to. It has been hard, though, to find close friends. There are very few Tanzanians that share the same values that I do or have the same concerns. This has made it somewhat difficult and disappointing. Yet, I continue to enjoy the people and my work. I get a great deal of support from my friends, but most of my support comes from God.

It is interesting to live with Muslims. At times, their religion seems a bit legalistic to me, yet I do hope to learn more about them and their faith. Often times they seem to have much more respect for God than we do as Christians. To them, God is so great and untouchable that respect is of the utmost importance.

I find the Muslims, as with everyone, good people with a good sense of what is right and wrong. Yet, there is something inside me that wants to share with them the freedom that Christianity promises...

Part V

July 7, 1983 (Bi-annual Report)

I continue to enjoy the missionary lifestyle. The Tanzanians themselves play an important role in my adjusting to the environment. They are very supportive in that they are outgoing and also respectful. Tanzanians love to enjoy what little they have. I am learning a great deal from them.

Although I get encouragement from those around me, most of the support I receive come from Above me. I continue to grow closer to God and I am amazed by God constantly. Much of this is due to the lack of distractions here at Buhemba. There is plenty of time for meditation and reflection. This time is vital for mature growth. Without time to listen to God, it is very hard to reform bad habits and behavior. In fact, it would be very easy to settle into a comfortable and methodical association with the Lord. Although I tend to take advantage of many of my friendships, I do not want to exploit my relationship with Him.

In quiet times I have been able to give consideration to the concept of poverty and how development fits into that. Before serving the poor, it is important to know who they are. Raymond Fung in an article in 'The Other Side' (November 1982), says that the minimum condition which makes human life worthwhile is a family eating together. The poor are those that either do not have food or do not have a community to eat it with. He writes, "Policies, actions, governments and systems which enable families to eat together are good and those which prevent families from eating together are bad."

For families to buy food, jobs must be available. If the only job available is far away from the home village, (such as that of a massage parlor maid in a tourist city or a worker in a gold mine in South Africa), then to combat poverty is to combat unemployment, exploitation, and racist policies. If a family eats together knowing that the secret police can come and take away a member, then to combat poverty is to defend human rights.

Developed countries face a like definition of poverty. Even though there is plenty of food, if a person is alone and has no one to share it with, that person can be considered poor. Perhaps, as well, those families who do not find the time to sit together at the table to share a meal and talk with each other can be thought of as poor.

Before God, we are all developing people. Development cannot be evaluated only in technical and economic terms. Included might be sense of community, how foreigners are treated, how the disadvantaged are treated, and whether or not all people are treated as equals before God.

8 July 1983

My good friend Virginia,

Well, I have had your letter on my desk for too long now! I have been thinking a lot about you lately. I do hope you are in good spirits. I am sure you are as you have such a wonderful faith. God so richly blesses you. Well, He so richly bless us all. I want to thank you for your most beautiful letter and gift in my name. How did you know that the best gift a person can give me is to make a donation to a charitable organization? God takes care of all the material needs. You know that. Thank you, Virginia for our gift to the St. John's Children's Home for me. I am deeply touched by this gesture. Really, more people should express love for one another in this way. It is a simple and selfless way of telling a person that we are blessed with so much. In our thankfulness, we can help those who really need it.

I hope and pray that you are well Virginia. How is your family? Warm greetings to your grandfather. I hope and assume that he is well. Oh, you did say that he sent his kind regards to me, please thank him.

I am amazed and complimented by your simple and sincere warmth. Your letters always generate a real satisfaction, Virginia. I thought it was funny that the nuns keep offering you the opportunity to join them. That is a great compliment. You had mentioned that you had thought of becoming a nun, but that whatever you do, you want to do the right thing and the righteous thing. The funny part is, I have thought of being a priest too. I want to do the righteous thing. Although I am a Protestant, the Catholic Church intrigues me. So many remarkable people have come out of the Catholic Faith. Yet, I don't know if I would be able to change my own faith. Then I gave some thought to being a Protestant priest or monk – or something. I could even start my own order. I have not given up on the idea of marriage and having a family. In any event, being a priest or a religious, is a noble thing!

I believe the Lord has put me here to re-evaluate my values and relationships – a lot of soul searching.

Will you be going to the UWP reunion in Tucson? I would go, but my private jet is out of commission at the moment. If you should attend, please say hi to the folks for me, especially Christy Lamb.

Things here at Buhemba are going fairly well. The heifer breeding project is coming along. We actually got some materials. We have built some fences. The heifers should be coming soon. It is hard to believe, after all, I have only waited a year and 8 months! It is good that we are starting work. It makes me very busy which leaves little time for other things. Not that I regretted not having specific work because I have really enjoyed just spending time with the local people. It has been more rewarding, and it seems more productive than actual technical work.

I have been given some thoughts as to what I am going to do with the rest of my life. I feel that I am at a turning point. I need to know what I am going to do when I finish this term with the Mennonites. If I come back for another term, I feel that Tanzania would be a permanent part of my life. I am not sure I want that. My parents are moving out of Connecticut. So, I really won't have a "home" to go to. The States will be very different. I may go back for my Master's, but I don't know in what field. I could get financial aid, but I am thinking I might like to get a job and make some money. Security sounds nice. That could include getting married. Anyway, I need to trust God and leave it to Him.

Well Virginia, I must go to bed. I am falling asleep. I am getting embarrassed because I don't want you to think that I am bored writing to you.

Do take care dear friend.

Mungu Akubariki, Rafiki yangu

God Bless you my friend,

Love,

Mark

July 30, 1983 from Buhemba

I spent a good part of this past month getting over a fantastic case of Malaria. The usual dose of chloroquine had no effect. I had a terrible headache and fever and lost my appetite. I did not think that I had it, but the dispensary checked my blood and told me that I was 100% positive for Malaria. Unfortunately, the mosquitoes developed a strain of Malaria immune to chloroquine. So, we have gone back to quinine. It is the old-fashioned treatment, and it is effective, though it does have some side effects. There is a new drug called Fansidar but it is not available here. This new strain of Malaria poses a real problem here. I often think it might have been better not have been so free in handing out chloroquine every time one got a mild case of Malaria.

September 4, 1983 from Buhemba

I have plowed my small “shamba” and am waiting for steady rains before planting again. I hope to plant beans, peanuts and a little popcorn (for my own use). I feel a little guilty planting a specialty crop like popcorn that only the White people eat. If I plant beans and peanuts, then I feel I help the local people. I’ll plant just enough popcorn to fill my own needs.

Recently, I walked to Shirati, the Mennonite mission hospital. It is about 60 miles from Buhemba. It was quite a trip. I got to Musoma, thirty miles away, the first day, where I got a room in a hostel for the night. The next day, I took a shortcut through the bush. I was not too sure of the way and I got lost. It was kind of amazing. I had not met anyone on the path up to that point. When I realized that I was not where I should have been, I thought, "Okay Lord, I'd sure appreciate it if you could find someone to tell me if this the right way or not." Of course, within the next minute, some little kid came sauntering down the path. He directed me on the right way. There, I met up with a family who was going my way. I knew that I would not find a hostel in the middle of the boonies. Then, these people, who did not even know me, invited me to stay in their home for the night! They were so gracious. They gave up one of their few beds for me. They prepared a special meal for me and went out of their way to make me feel at home. The next day, they suggested that instead of going on, that I should stay there and rest. I thought, "Why not?" They were so hospitable. I was amazed. The next day, their son gave me a ride on his bicycle to the hospital. The Tanzanians are so generous and hospitable. We really have a lot to learn from them.

I only went to the hospital to visit the American Mennonites there. When I had arrived, it was just in time for the funeral of the Bishop's wife who had died the day before. There were over 2,000 people there, many milling around, outside the church. She was buried outside of the church which confirmed the fact that she was part of the church. The custom is to be buried in one's home village, but that would have been a sign that she felt closer to home than the church. A lot of folks, especially her family, were not happy about it.

I stayed there for a week. It was a good trip. I realized when I got there, that God had sent me there to be part of them. I was thankful to be there. I came home refreshed and ready to get back into the routine of things.

October 3, 1983 from Buhemba

Recently, I was lucky to get involved in a local "yowe" (yoe-way). It is the community's response to a theft, usually cattle. The victim lets out a very shrill call which is picked up and sounded throughout the village. The men set out in small groups to search for the cattle, armed with bows and poison-tipped arrows, machetes, and clubs. They will go all night if need be. If they get hungry, they will stop at any house and demand food. If that person is not involved in the yowe, he is obliged to contribute to it.

Stolen cattle are often herded across the Kenyan border where they can be sold for Kenyan shillings which are worth four times as much as the Tanzanian shilling. Often, the thieves are young guys. Depending on the tribe, a young man wanting to get married, has to offer 15 to 45 cows as the bride price. If he does not have them, he is tempted to steal them.

If the cattle are found, they are returned to the owner. The next day, he will slaughter one of them, and all those people who were involved, get a portion of the meat. In addition, if there is a household who did not help, something such as a table, a chicken or even a radio is confiscated from it. These things are auctioned off the same time that the meat is handed out. It shows the strong sense of community held by these people and the obligations that each person has toward it.

Things go well, but I have been kind of tired lately. I have yet to take a vacation this year and I am thinking that I need one. I have been finding myself getting colder toward people, less sensitive and a real crank. People have been getting on my nerves lately. I often wonder where I would be without The Lord's help. He is always there. I wish I could avail myself more to Him.

Yesterday, some Assembly of God folks came to visit me. They gave me quite a preaching about speaking in tongues and how one was not saved if he did not do it. I thought it was interesting that two Tanzanians would be telling me, a "missionary", that I needed to be saved! I enjoyed the fact that the local people are evangelizing and that we missionaries are NOT overlooked. We need to re-evaluate our position. It was a good opportunity to look at my lifestyle.

I certainly don't condemn the Charismatic Movement. Here in Tanzania most Charismatics are really decent people. They follow Christ's teachings, and they really live for Him. Most mainline churches have done a poor job at getting dedicated people. Most Christians do as they please and do not lead particularly moral lives. I am intrigued by the success of the Assembly of God church. Most churches here need some kind of renewal, but is speaking in tongues a requirement? Anyway, whatever the case, I am not ready for the Charismatic Movement.

October 27, 1983 from Shirati

I am on my way to Nairobi. I am taking a week's vacation to visit friends. It is also a time to be a real glutton as there is everything imaginable to buy there. It is a city much like a city in the states. It is ironic to find so much available in such a poor country. Anyway, it should be a good time to relax and to pig out on chocolate, ice cream and the rich man's life.

B.R.A.C.
BOX 160
MUSOMA, TANZANIA
TANZANIA 1/-
TANZANIA 1/-
moo!
MUSOMA
TANZANIA
AIRMAIL
MISS VIRGINIA LAPOINTE
20 CARILLON RD.
TICONDEROGA, N.Y. 12883
USA
TANZANIA 1/-

Nov. 1983

Dear Virginia,

Thank you for your very good letter.

Is Buckam Kiru your friend? How did you meet him?

Thank you for sending me your friend Karen Ryan's address. God love her for serving in The Peace Corps. She is most welcome to come and visit me here in Tanzania. A friend of yours is a friend of mine and especially one from your same hometown. Who knows, maybe I will even get to Zaire!

Thank you for that article on celibacy. It came at a time when I was feeling particularly lonely. 99% of the Tanzanians are freer with sex than the Americans. Friends between men and women do it as casual as anything. Christians are just as bad as non-Christians. Sometimes I wonder, but I am convinced that abstaining is the Christian thing to do. "The noblest manifestation of power is the ability not to use it." I will hang on to this article.

Things here go on as usual. I am constantly being amazed by God and His Goodness. The Tanzanians also do a good job of amazing me and keeping me entertained. They are very joyous in their living.

Finally, we have gotten 25 of the 50 heifers that we need for the heifer breeding project. We will be getting the other 25 as soon as diesel if more available. Fuel shortages are a major problem here. We also have a lot of other things that we need to get yet. I am not too sure that the project will be finished by the time I am supposed to come home. It takes so long to get anything done here. As far as work goes, I am not getting a lot of experience. As a Christian, and as a human being, I have grown a lot. I guess that is more important than work experience. I keep telling myself that anyway!

Well Virginia, I can't think of anything else to say. There is not much going on at all. I only hope and pray that you are well. You must be exhausted after your trip to China. Please tell me all about it. You really have done a lot. You will certainly have a lot to write about in your book.

Please say hi to your grandfather for me. Do take care of yourself as well as others, Virginia. God Bless you.

Lots of Love,

Virginia

Nov. 1983

Dear Virginia,

Thank you for your great letter. Wow! That sure is interesting. The people in China seem to be very oppressed. At least here, the people have a relatively decent amount of freedom. Maybe it is because China is so heavily populated, they cannot have the same freedoms. I sent away for a Chinese magazine, but I have not received it yet. I have also sent you a subscription. I hope you get it alright. It has fantastic pictures of China in it. Let me know if you get it as many times in the Third World, one orders something and never gets it. So, pray!

Things are well here. I leave in November. That is not much time. I find myself becoming more and more anxious to get home and to see family; to get on with life, etc. I love Tanzania and I think that I will return some day. I think now that I am getting a bit worn around the edges.

wrote to you, I was at a low point at my existence here. Though I have not quite recovered, I am not at the same low point.

The one thing that affects me so much is the uncertainty of my future. Yet, all my strength comes from Above. Does all that 'gobble-dee-gook" make sense?

The project goes slowly. We have 34 heifers now. We want 75. We have yet to get the bulls. So obviously, the project will not be finished in November of 1984 when I leave. There are many reasons for the failure. Perhaps I am part of the reason to blame. The biggest problem is that Tanzania is poor and made that much more poor, due to the Socialist government. There is nothing available. So, the needed infrastructure has to be built. (I am sitting here waiting for someone and some other guy told me that all Africans say hi to you!).

So, there is not much happening here, and you must get tired of hearing of the same old stuff. I have just been here at Buhemba, living each day and enjoying myself. This past week, I had a guest which was nice. He was a Tanzanian. I get lonely living by myself. It was nice to have the company. I have not been able to do much traveling. I would like to, but I get the impression that they don't like me traveling. Psychologically, I find that I need to get away once in a while. The people at Buhemba are nice, but to work here, and have no change is a lot for me. Anyway, that is life.

So sorry this is such a terrible letter. Tell me more about you! I care about you and I want you to be happy.

Well, my very good friend, I pray that you are well and enjoying those around you. I know those around you enjoy you. Take care of yourself Virginia. I know you spend so much of your time serving others. God Bless you.

Love,

Mark

December 12, 1983

Heri ya Sikukuu

Dear Virginia,

Howdy! I have your postcard in front of me. Boy you sure do get around. China must have been fantastic! I would love to get to China and see The Great Wall, and all the sights. Which city did you like best? How long were you there for? What did you do? Were you with a group? Are you able to get credit for the experience?

Please, Virginia, write and tell me all about it. It must have been beyond amazing!

Before I go on, please let me wish you a Belated Merry Christmas! I know it is late. It has been really hard for me to get things done lately. Anyway, I sure do wish that you had a real special holiday. How is your family? Please tell them that I said Hello, especially your grandfather. I really hope that your Christmas was special and Blessed. I am sure it was as you were away from home last Christmas. Did it snow in Ticonderoga? I sure bet it is beautiful!

I will be spending Christmas quietly at Buhemba with one other missionary couple. They are a really nice elderly couple from New Zealand. They are Anglican. It should be nice, though it sure won't feel like Christmas here. I miss the cold, the music, the decorations and all of that. Without it, it does not really feel like Christmas. The important thing is why we celebrate Christmas which is the greatest thing ever that happened. I will be praying for you on the holiday, and I know that my prayers will be answered.

I have been really busy lately, but I have not been able to get much done as far as work goes. I am almost positive that the heifer breeding project will not be done by the time that I leave next November. I am growing weary as there is not much to do at Buhemba. It has taken two years to get some practical work done. Anyway, what the heck.

The Tanzanians are really nice folk, and they keep me entertained. We hopefully will be getting some bulls for breeding purposes. There is so much to do.

Right now, I am in Kenya for a retreat. There are people from six different countries here from all over East Africa. It 's a pretty good time. I really needed to get out of Buhemba this year. I have been really tired. It is a good time to get together with different people to see what everyone is doing. It is very easy to get lost in my own little world at Buhemba. There are some really interesting and creative people here. There is time to sing, play sports, and relax and sleep and just get away. I can use one of these retreats once a month! Now that the Tanzanian border has been opened, it is a lot easier to get here than it used to be.

Well, Virginia, I better get going. I hope that you are doing well and are happy. I pray that you have a really special holiday with your family.

Do take care and God Bless you.

Love,

Mark

Part VI

January 2, 1984 from Buhemba

It has been an interesting year. I have really learned a lot and have changed. I guess we all do.

Not much has happened with the project. I am finally becoming a bit tired and frustrated about it. It would be nice to be able to say that I got something done while I was here. Yet, I know that God is not so much concerned with quantity as quality of life. I guess it is the pressure of all the people that makes me feel as if life has to be filled with all kinds of projects and stuff. Anyway, I hope that I can get it pretty much on its way by the time I leave.

Yet, I think that I have learned a lot about the world and the situation that it is in. It is amazing how we Americans get these weird ideas on how the world should be running by just sitting and watching the TV. Perhaps TV is really running the world!

February 22, 1984 from Buhemba

When I go home, I think I will be a lot different from the average American Christian. It will be hard for me to adjust to them. I mean this half of the world is materially in a hole all their lives. To go rich Christians crying poor s they wonder where thy are going to get money to buy a new LTD car will be quite a switch! I have seen a lot in what Christ says about the rich and the poor. He is so right when He talks about camels and needles. I have the impression that the door to Heaven is not "pearly gates" at all. The door is a needle hole. The real camels are not in the Sahara as we might think. Europe, the U.S., and the rest of the secular West is where the real camels live. I wonder if I can handle that. I'd like to dedicate myself to being poor. The idea scares me.

Being poor materially means giving up one's security. That's what real poverty is. Sure, it would be fun to be poor, but what do I do when I am seventy and can't make money? (Now I know why Africans have so many children!) But real wealth comes from the security of God. It comes through faith. One can be as poor as anything and be one of the richest people in the world. And one can have twelve cars, sixteen houses, four yachts and tons of cash and be one of the poorest because faith is only in things. Generally, the richer one is with things, the poorer one is spiritually. So, going back home kind of scares me.

I remain confused about my future. Yet, the super part is that I'm not pulling my hair out with worry. I know God will take care of it. I used to know the next step in my life. Now, I have got to get that security from some place else. Maybe I can call it relying on God. This all kind of sounds hairy, but what the heck – Jesus probably sounded like that to His listeners. So, no decisions on the future. I am not comfortable with it; yet, in a way, I am.

March 28th, 1984 from Buhemba

The past few weeks have been very difficult for me. The project just does not seem to be able to get off the ground. Besides, being a “Mennonite” on a government project living at an Anglican center has meant real confusion as to who is boss. But I have had virtually nothing to do for two and a half years. It seems that the last part of my term will be equally useless. I mean that in a technical sense. It has been a great growing experience for sure. I admit that part of the fault lies within myself. But it is not all my fault! The system here is very difficult to work under as nothing is available, and the government is so inefficient. I feel tired, worn, burned out and useless as a missionary. But I am not worried about my spirituality, or about Heaven. It is this earthly existence that has thrown me off.

March 7, 1984 Bi-Annual Report

Lately, I've been contemplating the concept of development in today's world. It is a game where the rich are the players, and the poor are the pawns. After twenty years of development programs, the poor are poorer than ever before. Today's situation appears hopeless. Time is running out.

If the rich were really interested in changing the lives of the poor, they would be willing to give up more of what they hoard. There just isn't enough wealth in the world for everyone to be affluent. Nyerere calls for a New Economic Order. This makes sense. The world system isn't fair.

What is development anyway? Christ had an answer. He talked about real food and real drink. In John 6: 53-58, He calls Himself the Real Sustenance of life. Bread and water bring temporary relief, but Christ brings permanent satisfaction. He didn't bring promises of great wealth and a softer way of life. What He brought was the ultimate in development projects. Christ brought to the poor self-worth. He taught self-conscientization and liberation. He illustrated racial and sexual equality. He changed attitude and created hope for the hopeless.

Part VII

Mark's Work is Finished

April 5, 1984 from Buhemba – *The Final Letter*

Happy Easter! Let it be a super time and full of real meaning.

To my Dear friend Mark,

Who is as gentle as a Lamb – like our Lord.

May our Risen Savior bless you
In His most gracious way
With all the joy and promise
Of this happy Easter Day
And all throughout your future
May His precious love impart
A world of ever-growing faith
To dwell within your heart.

Lovingly,
Virginia
XOXO

18 April 1984

Easter Blessings

Then one day, one of my letters was returned to me. It was the Easter card that I had sent out on April 18, 1984. With it, was the following letter:

Dear Virginia,

I am so sorry to have to write to you and give you the very sad news about our son Mark. I do feel that you need to be informed.

On April 18, 1984, Mark fell 25 feet from a water tower while doing routine work. He was killed almost instantly. It was quite a shock to

Burt and me and all who knew him. We have had so much support and Christian love shown to us that we have been able to continue our lives from one day to another. It has been very difficult to do a lot of writing, but I wanted to send your letters with a small amount of information about Mark.

If you ever get down this way, please come for a visit.

God Bless,

Burt and Sue Day

I was shaking when the packet arrived in the mail, and now, nearly 40 years later I am consumed with grief once again. I feel that everyone should know of Mark Edward Day's legacy though this has been emotionally draining to write. I have never known a love quite like his.

Our mutual friend Christy Lamb described Mark best when she nominated him for 'Up With

People's Everyday Hero' presented posthumously at our ten year reunion.

"I want to paint a picture of Mark as the down to earth, approachable person he was and not to immortalize him as is easy to do when we lose a person so dear. Imagine Mark before us with his unassuming stance and broad, goofy grin across his face. He was small of stature and easy to overlook in a crowd, but I remember his big strong hands (he was my dance partner you see). I would often get frustrated with Mark for not paying attention to the dance steps that we were being taught in rehearsals. He seemed to be in another world. Later, in a letter, Mark told me that he was bored during those rehearsals. I wish I could offer a penny for his thoughts during those times. I suspect his thoughts were of a very deep nature.

"Mark is the least materialistic person I've ever met. In the words of Rev. Peirce,

'Mark's love for people was accompanied by a disregard for material things. This is a significant sign of the Christ-presence ignored by so many Christians. We live in a culture that puts a premium on the material and degrades the personal as less worthy. The successful person is defined as the accumulator of wealth. Mark would be defined as a failure by that culture. But we who love Christ, know that 'the mystery' revealed in Mark – his deep love of and concern for people – mark his as a person whose name is written large at the top of the page of 'The Book of Life' (Revelation 3:5).'

Mark was 26 years old when he died that Holy Week.

Something small to remember one great – a weeping (appropriately enough) cherry tree planted at the church.

Donec iterum conveniant

www.ingramcontent.com/pod-product-compliance
Ingram Content Group UK Ltd.
Pitfield, Milton Keynes, MK11 3LW, UK
UKHW041639190726
13854UKWH00006B/2586

9 798746 586759